The YOUth Are Our Future© Copyright 2021 by Poetic Life Allah (Herr Jeff)

No part of this publication may be reproduced, distributed, or transmitted in any form or by any means, including photocopying, recording, or other electronic or mechanical methods, without the prior written permission of the publisher, except in the case of brief quotations embodied in critical reviews and certain other noncommercial uses permitted by copyright law. All rights reserved.

This is a work of fiction. Names, characters, businesses, places, events, locales, and incidents are either the products of the author's imagination or used in a fictitious manner. Any resemblance to actual persons, living or dead, or actual events is purely coincidental. For permission requests, write to the author, addressed: "Attention: Permissions Coordinator," at the address below.

Infinity Publications, LLC.

Vanderbilt Media House, LLC.

999 Waterside Drive

Suite 110

Norfolk, VA 23510

(804) 286-6567

Word Up I Children Press is a subsidiary of Infinity Publishing Group, Inc.

Infinity Publications, LLC.

Illustrated by David Hill

ISBN-13 : 978-1-953096-02-9

First Edition : December 2021

10 9 8 7 6 5 4 3 2 1

www.vanderbiltmediahouse.net

This book was printed in the United States

Dedication:

This book is dedicated to all our YOUth who when given the resources and opportunity can and will bring forth beautification beyond our imagination. I dedicate this book to my nieces and nephews: Kiara, Aaron, Ramik, Katie, Shawn Lamont, Vaughn, Zania, Dylan, Dakarai, Simarai, Miracle, and Kingsington. To all of YOU, and to Justice, Jade, Dameir, and Nevaeh; know that I see the greatness inside YOU and that YOU can be whatever YOU want and do whatever YOU want if you work hard and believe in yourself.

Acknowledgements:

I would like to show my thanks and appreciation for Allah The Father (Hon. Clarence Edward Smith) who gave all that he had and did all in his power to make sure the youth received and understood the value of true education. It is because of his equality and his sacrifice that I understand that the wealth of any country is the children not the money. Because of his teachings and his sacrifice, I am a better student, teacher, brother, and man. Thank you, Allah, Justice, and all those who learned what he taught and taught what they learned.

There are so many people over the years who have taught me, inspired me, supported me, motivated me, and loved me, which all played a role in the creation of this book. If you think your name should be listed here and it is not, I promise this is not the last book and I will make up for it on the next one. Or you thought wrong. First and foremost, to my phenomenal Mother who has been there for me since the very beginning and has never wavered in her support or love. Thank you for everything and I promise to always be the type of Man you can be proud of. Thank you to Christopher (Life) and April Willars, Kya and Chauncey, Lord Prince, Lord Kalim, Lord Serious, Sahkeem (Paul Taylor), Hasan, God Shamod, Almighty, Aunt Sylvia, Determination, Knowso, I Be, Cee Myself, Magnetic Peace, Ambo, Jovan Haskell, Lil Bobby, Kataya, Rahim, Ms. Rawlings, Black Child, LaTron Huggins, King Just, Infinite Illumination, True Star, Father Sun, Lord Sincere (I can never thank you enough), Andre, Jody, Carlton, Vito (John Amos), Born Ruler, Sincere (Boston), Rell, Choice, Reborn (Marly Mall), Illaha, Lord Unique, Superior, Master C, Outstanding, Eternal, Lord Science, Black Darkness, Hakeem, and Divine War. Last and certainly not least, to the woman who really helped me make my idea a reality. She has supported and motivated me through this whole process by doing many of the things I was physically unable to do. I am forever grateful for her presence in my life. Thank you, Ms. Erika Latisha Holliday AKA Beautiful Queen Mecca.

This Book Belongs To:

_____

The YOUth are our future. These words are so true;

Because the future that lies ahead is all up to YOU.

The world can be a tough place but education is the key;
To shape and mold the world the way it should be.

The things that YOU learn and the things that YOU do;
Is the way that your world gets contributed to.

Two ways to make sure that YOU have an effect;

Is to work well with others and the jobs YOU select.

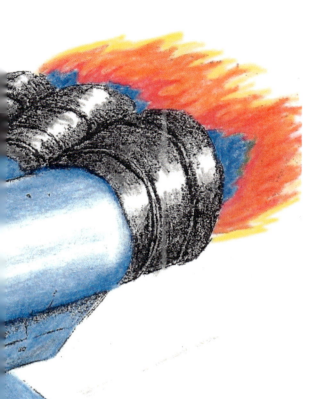

When YOU work well with others,
YOU strengthen the whole;

The jobs YOU select help YOU reach the main goal.
There's no job too big and there's no job too small;
From a janitor to an architect we need them all.
We need professors and teachers that share what they know;
We need farmers who plant crops and help them to grow.
We need pilots for planes and captains for ships;
We need conductors for trains when taking long trips.

There's so many jobs that we need YOU to take;
Like being a governor who runs a whole state.
Or the mayor of a city like the one where YOU live;
Or a pediatrician who's a doctor for kids.
Meteorologists study the weather and air;
Or YOU can be a judge who knows how to be tough, but fair.
We need detectives who investigate when people go missing;
When your laptop is broken you'll need a computer technician.

Astronomers are people who study the stars;
Congressmen meet and then come up with laws.
A tailor can fix up your clothes when they're torn;
An obstetrician is a person who helps babies be born.
Genealogists study genes and I'm not talking about clothes;
I mean the genes that determine your skin color and nose.
We need lawyers and authors and journalists too;
Who can research the truth and report it to YOU.

Archaeologists dig up clues from out of the ground;
That tells us how our ancestors were living when they were around.
Electricians and surgeons I have to include;
Plus dieticians who can show us the healthiest foods.
Biologists study life from people to ants;
Herbalists make medicine out of the plants.
YOU can be a brick mason who learns to build homes;
Or YOU can be a bank manager who gives people loans.

We need some inventors who create things in their mind;

Then our engineers will help make the designs.

Like engines for cars and motors for drones;

We'll also need soldiers to protect what we own.

If YOU work together there's no way YOU will fail;

What we don't need is more YOUth in prison or jail.

The last thing I'll say and these words are so true;

The most important part of the YOUth is YOU!

GLOSSARY

1. **Archaeologist-** person who studies ancient cultures by examining the remains that they dig up out of the ground.
2. **Architect-** person who designs buildings and directs their construction.
3. **Astronomer-** a person who studies the objects in outer space.
4. **Author-** a person who writes a novel, poem, essay, etc.
5. **Bank Manager-** a person who manages or works for a bank.
6. **Biologists-** a person who studies living things especially how they begin, grow, reproduce and how they are structured.
7. **Computer Technician-** a person who knows how computers work and how to fix them.
8. **Captain-** the commander of a ship.
9. **Conductor-** the person in charge of a railroad train, bus, or streetcar.
10. **Congressman-** a member of the U.S. Congress who as a group of people discuss, arrange, and promote laws for their state.
11. **Detective-** a member of the police force, whose job is to gain information and evidence in criminal cases.
12. **Dietician-** a person who knows the quality and effects of food and knows how to plan and supervise meals.

13. **Electrician-** a person who installs, operates, maintains, or repairs electrical devices.
15. **Engineer-** a person trained to design, build and use engines or machines.
16. **Farmer-** a person who operates a farm or works to raise grain, fruits and vegetables from the land.
17. **Genealogist-** a person who studies family history by tracing where people come from through their parents, grandparents, etc.
18. **Governor-** the person who is elected to direct and control the operations of a state.
19. **Herbalist-** a person who is an expert in herbs and plants, especially as medicine.
20. **Inventor-** a person who created a new appliance, machine, or way of doing something.
21. **Janitor-** a person who takes care of and cleans up a building or office.
22. **Journalist-** a person who writes or edits for a newspaper or magazine.
23. **Judge-** a person whose job is to decide right and wrong in a court of law and what the punishment or reward should be.
24. **Lawyer-** a person who gives legal advice, help and representation.
25. **Mayor-** a person who is elected to direct and control the operation of a city.

26. Meteorologist- a person who studies the atmosphere and the things that go on there, especially the weather.

27. Obstetrician- a person trained to treat women in childbirth before and after delivery.

28. Pediatrician- a person trained to treat the medical, hygienic needs or diseases of children.

29. Pilot- a person trained to fly an airplane, balloon, or other aircraft.

30. Professor- a person who teaches in a college or university.

31. Soldier- a person who serves in an army or military.

32. Surgeon- a person who treats diseases or injuries by operating on people.

33. Tailor- a person who makes or repairs clothing.

34. Teacher- a person who gives knowledge, instructions, or skills to another.

Archaeologist

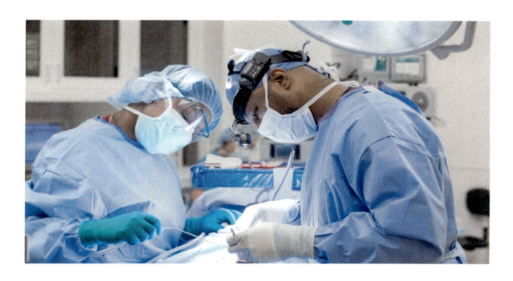

Surgeon

Teacher

Politican

Gynocologist

Pilot

17

Soldier

Janitor

Conductor

Astronomer

Detective

Brick Mason

Black History

The first Black person in Congress (U.S. Senator) was Hiram Rhodes Revels. He was elected by the Mississippi legislature on Jan. 20, 1870 and was seated on Feb. 25, 1870.

The first Black woman in Congress was Shirley Chisholm. She was elected on Nov. 5, 1968.

The first Black governor was P.B.S. Pinchback, who became governor of Louisiana on Dec. 9, 1872. The first Black woman named to the cabinet of a U.S. president was Patricia R. Harris. She was named

Secretary of the Department of Housing and Urban Development by President Jimmy Carter on Dec. 21, 1976.

The first Black movie production company was the Lincoln Motion Picture Company. It was founded in Los Angeles in 1915 by two Black actors by the names of Clarence Brooks and Noble Johnson, a Black druggist named James T. Smith and a white cameraman named Harry Grant.

The first Black person with their own network radio show was Nat King Cole in 1945-46. He was also the first Black person with his own network TV show in 1956-57.

The first Black judge was Jonathan Jasper Weight. He was elected to the South Carolina Supreme Court on Feb. 1, 1870.

The first Black Supreme Court justice was Thurgood Marshall who was confirmed by the Senate on Aug. 30, 1967.

The first Black woman judge was Jane Matilda Bolin. She was appointed judge of the court of domestic relations of New York on July 22, 1939.

The first Black physician was James Dedham who was born a slave in 1767. In 1783, he bought his freedom and established a practice among blacks and whites. He was one of the leading physicians in New Orleans by 1788.

The first Black women physicians were Rebecca Cole, who practiced from 1872-1881; Susan McKinney and Rebecca Lee-Crumpler.

The first Black lawyer was Macon B. Allen. He practiced in Maine in 1843 and 1844. He was formally admitted to the bar on May 3, 1845.

The first Black woman lawyer was Charlotte E. Ray. She graduated from Howard University Law School on Feb. 27, 1872. She was admitted to practice in April 1872.

The first successful operation on the human heart was performed by Dr. Daniel Hale Williams on July 9, 1893 at Chicago's Provident Hospital.

The first Black person to receive a degree from an American college was Lemuel Haynes.

The first Black person to receive a Ph.D. degree was Patrick Francis Healy. He passed the final examination at Louvain in Belgium on July 25, 1865.

The first Black person to receive a Ph.D. from an American University was Edward A. Boucher. He earned a degree in physics at Yale in 1874.

The first Black woman to graduate from an American college was Mary Jane Patterson. She graduated from Oberlin College in 1862.

The first Black woman to receive a Ph.D. was Sadie M Alexander. She received a degree in economics from the University of Pennsylvania in 1921.

The first Black general was Maj. Gen. Robert B. Elliot, commanding general, National Guard, South Carolina (1870).

The first Black general in the regular army was B.O. Davis Sr. He was appointed by President Franklin Delano Roosevelt on Oct. 16, 1940.

The first Black general in the U.S. Air force was B.O. Davis Jr. He was appointed on Oct. 27, 1954.

The first Black woman general was Hazel Johnson. She was appointed on Sept. 1, 1979.

The first Black woman to write a Broadway play was Lorraine Hansberry. She created Raisin In The Sun. It premiered on March 11, 1959.

The first Black woman millionaire was Madame C.J. Walker. She was one of the first major Black entrepreneurs. She owned and sold hair care and beauty products.

The first Black woman to head a bank was Maggie Lena Walker. She was named president of Richmond's St. Luke Bank and Trust Company in 1903.

The first Black woman nominated for President of the U.S. was Shirley Chisholm.

The first Black newspaper was Freedom's Journal and it was published in New York on March 16, 1827.

The first Black owned radio station was WERD. It went on air in Atlanta on Oct. 3, 1949. The first Black owned TV station, Detroit's WGPR-TV went on air on Sept. 29, 1975.

The first Black astronaut was Robert Henry Lawrence Jr. The first Black person to fly in space was Guidon S. Bluford.

The first Black woman astronaut and the first Black woman to fly in space was Mae Jemison.

The first Black President of the U.S was Barack Obama. The first Black Vice President of the U.S is Kamala Harris.

Made in the USA
Middletown, DE
22 December 2021

56921062R00015